Getting Along:
how to be happy
with yourself
and others

Getting Along:
how to be happy with yourself and others

Dr. J. H. Schmidt
as told to
Paul G. Neimark

G. P. Putnam's Sons · New York

Second Impression

Copyright © 1979 by Paul G. Neimark and Dr. J. H. Schmidt
All rights reserved.
Published simultaneously in Canada
by Longman Canada Limited, Toronto.
Printed in the United States of America
12 up

Library of Congress Cataloging in Publication Data
Neimark, Paul G
Getting along.
SUMMARY: Gives suggestions for and examples of ways
of getting along with others by learning to get along   .
with yourself.
1. Interpersonal relations—Juvenile literature.
[1. Interpersonal relations] I. Schmidt, J. H.,
joint author. II. Title.
HM132.N43   301.11   78-14309
ISBN 0-399-20654-X

Contents

Getting Along:
how to be happy with yourself and others

1 Good Day—Bad Day

Lauri's Monday turned out to be a piece of cake. But it certainly didn't start that way.

First, her younger brother woke up sick with the flu, so *she* had to take out the dog. Second, Lauri's mother was in a bad mood because now she had to stay home and take care of Jimmy, putting off the shopping and missing her first racquetball lesson.

"Mom," Lauri asked, "where's the big frying pan?"

Her mother yelled the answer angrily.

To top it all off, when Lauri arrived at school, the teacher in first class had brought in a guest speaker who talked for the entire hour. Yet this was the day Lauri had been scheduled to give her own report to the class—a report she'd worked on every night for three weeks so it could be as close to perfect as possible.

Lauri had started out the day with swelling spirits. Though a little wind was taken out of her sails at home, now she felt as if her balloon had burst completely. What a disappointment!

And yet, Lauri's Monday turned out to be a piece of cake. How?

Because Lauri knew how to *get along*. Especially outside her home. Some things that go wrong in your home can't be helped. But she had learned how to make the world outside a happy place for herself. And so, when things didn't go just right at home, Lauri was able to deal with them better.

Bert, on the other hand, had a rough day.

It started off all right. His favorite breakfast, blueberry pancakes, was waiting for him on the breakfast table. And then he was lucky enough to get a ride to school. But little by little after that, everything seemed to go wrong.

Not that there was any one big thing he could put his finger on. First, he passed Charlie in the hall on the way to his first class, and asked how the wrestling meet came out.

"We lost by two points," Charlie answered.

"You *lost*? To Overland Park?" Bert said. "You guys should've slaughtered them!"

Charlie just nodded, feeling bad about the whole thing again, and walked on. "See you at the pinball parlor?" Bert shouted.

"No"—Charlie threw over his shoulder—"not today. See you later."

And then he was gone, leaving Bert feeling a little bit bad

himself, though he wasn't sure why. Except that he wanted to be a closer friend of Charlie's, but had never quite been able to do it.

However, Bert didn't stop to think about that short conversation until later on, when he began to see that the whole day was becoming a mess. At lunch, for instance, there was only one meat-in-cabbage left in the cafeteria, and just as he was about to take it, he saw that the girl next in line had the same idea. Bert wanted to turn to her and say, "Hey—you look like you were going to have this, and it really doesn't make all that much difference to me. Here, take it."

But instead, for some reason, he didn't say anything. She was pretty, and maybe it could have been the start of his having a girlfriend. "Well, too late now," he thought. But it did bother him, and maybe that was why he got in trouble with his English teacher next period.

When Bert walked into Mr. Taylor's class, he saw two empty seats. One was near the front between a couple of people he didn't know too well. The other was in the back row next to a bunch of fellows who were in danger of failing the course. One of them waved for him to come over and sit down. Bert hesitated a minute, then did. About halfway through the period, Oscar (the fellow who had waved to Bert) wrote a four-letter word on the shirt of the boy next to him. When the guy saw what was happening, he started to write on Oscar's arm. Unfortunately, Bert was sitting between them. He was called into the principal's office with them.

After that, Bert knew the day was going downhill. So, instead of getting his homework done right after school, he watched TV—a couple of programs he didn't even like. Later, with four hours of homework staring him in the face and a whole day in which nothing good had really happened, Bert decided he'd play half an hour of pinball before hitting the books.

He walked over to the pinball parlor, but stayed too long and that put him in a worse mood. So, when a couple of fellows who were always looking for trouble came along, he gave it to them. The owner told all three of them not to come in again.

It had been a truly bad day for Bert.

And yet it had started off well. It had gone bad—as so many other days had for him—*because he didn't know how to get along.*

Where and how did Bert go wrong each time?

Even more important, what did Lauri know—and what did she do—about getting along with others that changed her day from a burst balloon into a piece of cake?

2 The Groundwork

First of all, Lauri laid the groundwork for a good day by not letting a bad beginning make all the difference.

Like anyone her age, Lauri felt her family was very important to her. But her school and her friends and her social life were becoming more and more important every day. After all, she spent more waking hours away than she did at home.

So the hour or less that she spent with her family in the morning wasn't an hour that she was going to let spoil the next ten or twelve. Before Lauri learned how to get along, she would have told herself: "My parents just don't understand me! Or else, why would Dad tell me to take the dog out after I had fixed my hair, and why would Mom yell at me for just asking a simple question?"

Lauri didn't feel her parents understood her one hundred

percent even now. But *she* understood *them* better, if not completely. She knew, for instance, that Dad had a big meeting today and had to make that 7:53 train. And she knew that getting the marketing done on schedule was important to Mom.

"But why do I have to come in second?" Lauri used to ask herself. Now, she saw that she would actually come in first by temporarily putting herself second.

Was it really a big deal taking out the dog? Or that her Mom—"who I know loves me"—yelled at her?

There *were* things where Lauri would stand her ground, but these today were not big deals. They would be, though, if she made them into that. Especially when she came home later, with homework to do, wanting to talk to her boyfriend, Jim, on the phone alone, and maybe have a couple of the girls over so they could plan a slumber party.

So, though she was tempted to make a scene, Lauri simply decided to get along with her family that Monday morning.

When she got home for dinner, it reaped some rewards. Her mother apologized for yelling, and her kid brother— who suddenly had recovered from his flu—didn't try to hog the TV as much.

Getting along is sometimes . . . simply *getting along*. That's all that Lauri had really done at home that morning. But how had she done it? What had gone on inside her that made the difference and reaped the rewards later?

It was a little trick she'd learned, Lauri's own secret. She called it "Turning the Boat Around." What that meant merely was that sometimes "the Boat," her day, got turned in the wrong direction. So she turned it around!

But it doesn't matter whether you call it Turning the Boat Around as Lauri does, or Beginning Your Day Over Whenever You Feel Like It (which is really what she was doing).

What does matter is that everyone who learns how to get along like this takes pretty much the same steps that Lauri did.

First, she recognized that things weren't going right. Obvious? You'd be surprised how many people, when something goes wrong early in their morning, let their mood be ruined for hours or even the whole day by never identifying what first got them "out of bed on the wrong side." Really, it wasn't when they got out of bed, was it?

Second, after Lauri realized things weren't going right, she quickly asked herself why. Was it her fault? No. But if it had been, by figuring it out right away, she could have done whatever was needed to make it right.

Was it something that just couldn't be avoided? No. But if it were, she could say to herself, "Well, there's nothing I could do about that. And it's not so terrible. Onward!"

But because Lauri had learned how to get along, most things that went wrong for her happened because someone else wasn't getting along. This was why her mother got angry at her for no reason at all. "Maybe Mom forgot to say to herself, 'I couldn't help Junior getting sick,'" Lauri thought.

But let's stop right here for a minute. You may have

been thinking to yourself, "These are such little things!"

And so they are. Just as the alphabet seems like such a simple little thing to you now. But unless you know your ABC's, you can't read or write. By the same token, though the differences between what Lauri and Bert thought and said in similar situations *were* small differences, *those differences . . . made all the difference.*

In this case, Lauri said nothing.

Because what she decided to do—the third step Lauri always took when something went wrong—was to go on with her day.

What could she do? Bert felt uneasy about his conversation with Charlie, but didn't stop to recognize that something had really gone wrong and so he could only come back later to "do" something about it. But Lauri had a choice right then and there. She could refuse to take the dog out, and get angry right back at her mother. She could take the dog out but, when her mother got angry for no reason, could tell her something like, "Look, Mom, this is too much. I think I deserve an apology."

Or, there was still another road she could have taken. She could give in to whatever happened and tell herself: "That's just the way my life is. I'm a victim of circumstances."

Lauri chose a fourth way. She *didn't* accept the situation in her mind, didn't like it, but decided it was best to say nothing then, get off to school and pretty much start the day over again—this time *better!* Yet let's stop for a moment and ask a question: If she *hadn't* decided that, how would you rate the other three ways of dealing with having to take the dog out when it wasn't her responsibility and being yelled at for no good reason?

Strange as it might seem, the last alternative is by far the worst. Many people think that you get along best by never making any trouble and giving in to just about everything that goes against you. But that's not really getting along, for you will begin to feel like a victim. Also, people will recognize that you always give in, and many of them will push you further and further. You don't need to be a victim. You have a choice.

And what if Lauri's choice had been to lose her temper, as her mother had done? Once in a while, that's not an unhealthy response, either. After all, it's only human to lose our tempers once now and then, especially in a frustrating situation someone else has brought about. Most doctors today agree that people who never lose their tempers often express their anger in "masked," unhealthy ways, such as feeling depressed.

So Lauri wasn't someone who never lost her temper. On the other hand, she didn't make a habit of it. And since she understood that people do lose their tempers once in a while, she understood that was what had happened with her mother.

Yet she could have taken the third course of going to Mom and saying, "Look—this is too much. I think I deserve an apology." And often, that *is* the best thing to do. It allows you to take a stand without standing (or stepping) on someone.

[19]

On another day, Lauri more than likely might have chosen that alternative. Why didn't she this Monday morning?

Partly because it was Monday morning and she was looking forward to her first class more than usual. She didn't want to take the time, especially when her mother was in a bad mood, to talk things out then and there and make herself even later. The other alternatives would still be open to Lauri later.

As it turned out, she didn't need them, because her mother came to her and apologized. Lauri couldn't know that at ten to eight in the morning, of course. But what she did know was that she didn't want any minor irritations to stop her from getting to that first class and giving the report on which she'd worked so hard.

So, despite a "bad" first hour of the day, Lauri closed the door of the house quietly behind her and looked forward smilingly to a very *good* day.

3 Knowing What You Feel

When Lauri reached school and discovered to her disappointment that she couldn't read the report, what did she do? This was something that couldn't be changed. The hour was lost. The chance—for now, at least—was lost. And she'd worked so hard!

Sure, she could try to enjoy the hour as best she could, listen to the guest speaker and attempt to act as though nothing had happened. But something *had* happened. Her heart just wasn't in it.

This situation was different from the one at home. To get along, she had to do some of the same things she'd done an hour before, but also one or two new ones. In fact, the very first thing she had to know was this: *Getting along is different in different situations.*

The first thing that Lauri did which was the same as before was to *identify what she felt.*

"I am so disappointed," she told herself. "What a rotten break!"

Again, *why* is this so important—to know what you feel? Because, though you don't always have to tell others what you feel, if you're to get along with others afterward, *you first do have to know what you're feeling.* If, for instance, Lauri had tried to escape the pain and disappointment of not being able to be the "star" that day, the disappointment wouldn't have gone away. She probably would have taken it out on someone else. Maybe someone important. It wouldn't have been worth it.

So she *felt* the disappointment for a few minutes—keenly. But then she said to herself, "Well, what can I do about it now?"

Lauri made the best she could of the hour, listening pretty well at times and taking some notes on the outside chance there might be a test on it sometime. But she was really waiting for the end of the period, and she didn't blame herself for it. When class was dismissed, Lauri confronted the situation with honest emotion expressed through an honest question.

"Mr. Taylor," she said, "I was really looking forward to giving my report today. I'll be able to next time—or sometime—won't I?"

Frankly, Mr. Taylor said, he'd forgotten. He taught not only this class, but four others, and he too was only human.

"But yes," he assured Lauri, "you'll have an opportunity to give your report. How about this Thursday?"

Lauri went away still a little disappointed, but also more than a little happy. She still had the report to look forward to! She could polish it up even more. Also, though Lauri didn't know it, she had raised herself in Mr. Taylor's opinion by her forthright handling of the situation, by showing that she was interested in his class.

Now, if what happened at home plus her first period at school was all that you knew about Lauri, you might think that doing well in her schoolwork and getting along with her family were most of what mattered to her. Not so. Lauri *did* love her family, and she *did* like to do well at school. But nothing was more important than her friends— both boys and girls. One of the big reasons she'd learned how to get along so well at home and in schoolwork was to be totally "together" when it came time to get along with her peers.

That's where Lauri was truly a pro. And that's also why the rest of her day turned out to be a piece of cake. Take the very next thing that happened.

4 Turning the Day Around

The opportunity to turn the day around came almost right away. But for those unusual people who know how to get along the way Lauri did, opportunities to make things go right were almost always around.

This time, the opportunity came because Lauri was eager to get to her next class and start fresh. "What the heck," she told herself, "the day can start at nine thirty instead of a quarter to seven, can't it? Or a new day can start right now!"

She quickly got to her next classroom on the other side of the school, after smiling hello to some friends on the way, and was the first one inside. Immediately, as she was about to sit down, Lauri saw that Ms. Faulkner, the drama teacher who taught speech there the period before, had left her purse in the corner.

Lauri liked Ms. Faulkner. So much, in fact, that she'd tried out just the other day for a big part in the class play. It would mean three afternoons a week after school if she landed the part, and Lauri already had a lot to do. But liking Ms. Faulkner wasn't the only reason she'd tried out; Lauri always wondered if she had acting talent and wanted to find out.

So here was a chance. She sat down and thought out her schedule so that she could fit in the extra hours if she got the part.

Usually Lauri was an optimist, but there were three or four other girls who were pretty good. One of them, Sue, had a better chance, Lauri thought, because Sue had already taken acting lessons. Still, Lauri had a feeling that Ms. Faulkner, an enthusiastic, spontaneous, shoot-from-the-hip type of person, just might give the part to a less experienced student. In fact, the drama teacher's impulsiveness might have been what made her forget her purse today.

Anyway, Lauri grabbed the purse and ran out of the room to find Ms. Faulkner. She paused for a second to tell Joey, who had just walked in, what she was doing and ask him to let their teacher for this period, Mr. Haliburton, know why she would be late. Lauri finally found Ms. Faulkner talking to somebody near the gym. She was starting to walk down the long corridor toward the assembly hall.

"Miss Faulkner!"

The drama teacher turned. "Lauri! What—" Then Ms. Faulkner saw what Lauri was carrying.

"My purse! I knew I'd forgotten something! Sometimes I think I'd forget my head if it weren't attached to my neck. Thank you!"

Lauri smiled. "You're more than welcome. It was fun finding you. My day kind of started off blah—and it really picked me up to have this little adventure."

Ms. Faulkner started to say something, but then didn't. That was a habit of hers. She was always saying whatever she thought—but once in a while thought better of it on second thought. Yet just as often, like right now, she decided to go ahead anyway. "Do you know who you looked just like when you said that?"

"Who?"

"Cathy!"

For a moment, Lauri drew a blank. Then suddenly she exclaimed, "You mean Cathy in—"

"In the play!" Ms. Faulkner said. "And—" She began to say something else, but stopped again, giving it a second thought. Then she barged right ahead:

"And you know what? I don't see how I could give the part to anyone else, with you talking and smiling and looking so much like Cathy. I wasn't going to make this decision until the end of the day and post it on the bulletin board, but I've just cast the part. If you want it, it's yours. *You're* Cathy!"

"Oh, thank you!" Lauri exclaimed. "I can't wait to start rehearsing!"

"I know that most teachers wouldn't do this," Ms. Faulkner said, pausing for a moment, as she always did before coming out with something that was on her mind. "But I'm not most teachers."

Lauri hurried back to class, so happy she could hardly contain herself. She wondered if she hadn't been the first one in the room and found the purse and raced after Ms. Faulkner and had that "Cathy" look on her face if whether she would have won the part.

She'd probably never know. But one thing Lauri did know: If you were willing to try to change your day from *blah* to *rah!* you might catch the biggest fish in the ocean.

5 Some Bitter, Some Sweet

Once you Turn the Boat Around, it usually is smooth sailing.

Yes, there was a problem here and a problem there during the remainder of Lauri's day. But so many good things added up to more than balance them, that she was able to handle the problems with ease and go on to the next enjoyable experience.

What were some of those problems?

For one, she snagged the back of her sweater on something or somebody while hurrying through the hall just before lunch. It was the busiest time, with people packed almost like sardines moving to and from the lunchroom. It was her favorite sweater. She wore it today because she was to give her report. Lauri felt something pull in the back, heard a noise which sounded like *riiiiiiip*, and went to the nearest mirror to take a look. Sure enough, there was a rip about an inch and a half long in back at her shoulder!

Fortunately, she always carried some spare clothing in her locker for emergencies—someone could spill something on you in the lunchroom, for example—and she was able to make a quick change. Still, it would mean something extra to carry on the way home, as well as some sewing to do once she got there. It also made her late to lunch, and the table Lauri usually sat at was filled up. This meant she couldn't sit among the people she usually ate with.

Near the far end of the lunchroom, at a half-table in the corner hardly anyone chose, Lauri saw a girl sitting alone. The girl was a transfer student, Lauri had heard someone say last Thursday or Friday. She decided to sit with her.

"Hey, Lauri," somebody said as she passed one table. "We can make room for you!"

"No"—Lauri smiled—"you're almost through anyway. But thanks." She said thanks as though she meant it—which she did.

Lauri reached the table at the end of the dining hall. The other girl looked up with a nervous but anticipatory expression. "Mind if I sit with you?" Lauri asked.

"Not at all," the girl answered.

"I'm Lauri."

"I'm Renee."

"You're a transfer student, aren't you?" Lauri asked. The girl nodded. "Where do you hail from—and how come you moved?"

Even though there were only about ten minutes of

lunch left when Lauri reached the cafeteria, she had a new friend before the bell rang. Renee had been lonely in this new school, and she was grateful to Lauri for coming over and sitting next to her, though she didn't say it. But Lauri knew it by the way Renee said goodbye. "Lauri, I hope I see you again soon," she said.

"Me, too," Lauri replied, then was on to her next class. Lauri was the kind of girl who could always turn a torn sweater into a newly embroidered friendship.

Yet another minor problem came about because of something good that happened. Just as something going wrong could often be turned to your advantage, Lauri knew that good fortune also might carry a bit of the bittersweet to it.

Lauri had gone to the bulletin board before she left school to see her name listed as Cathy for that part in the play. The list was up and standing right next to Lauri was Sue—one of the other girls who had tried out.

Lauri could see that Sue had wanted the part a lot—was she trying to hold back tears? Lauri tried to hold back her own happiness at seeing her name there (which meant she had the part for sure!) because she knew it could only make Sue feel worse. But suddenly Sue turned to her and asked, "You're Lauri, aren't you? The one who got the part of Cathy?"

Lauri nodded. But she didn't know what to say.

"I think I was just as good as you were," Sue said suddenly.

"I—I think you were good too," Lauri stammered. "I guess I was just lucky. I can't say I'm unhappy. I wanted the part, like you did. But for what it's worth, I wish there were a way we could both be happy this time. I—"

Lauri stopped. She'd said what she honestly felt, but she really didn't know how to make something good out of this.

Sue managed a little smile. "Forget it," she said. "Forget I said anything, would you? I've just been kind of down lately, and this was the last straw. There were half a dozen of us who tried out, so I really only had a one out of six chance, right? Let's drop it." And she walked away.

Lauri still felt a twinge for Sue, but she was happy that she got the part! Yet she mentally filed that sometime she wanted to go out of her way to be nice to Sue, partly because of the way things worked out, and partly because she knew Sue would be a little jealous of her for a while.

But for now, Lauri simply had to accept the fact that another person—through no fault of her own—didn't much like her. And that there was nothing at the moment that she could do about it.

Getting along, once in a while, meant taking a little bit of bitter with the very, very sweet.

Probably it has occurred to you that Lauri is too good to be true.

Well, it's important for you to know two things. First, Lauri *is* exceptional. She has learned how to get along, particularly with her peers, and that's something that is unfortunately all too rare today. In fact, it's pretty rare among adults.

But particularly with young people, something important to keep in mind is, in the beginning, anyway, that getting along *should* be the exception rather than the rule.

Why?

For one thing, growing up is a time of change, of some turbulence. The preadolescent and adolescent young man and woman are having all kinds of new feelings, experiencing all kinds of new stimuli thrown at them from the outside as well as from inside. Some seem to contradict others and must be sorted out. Ways of dealing with this new time of life must be learned, sometimes through trial and error.

So, getting along *isn't* automatic.

Sure, there are those one-in-a-thousand people who just seem to know how to get along from the time they are knee high. But did you ever stop to think that perhaps they merely learned it earlier? And even if there is that rare one-in-a-million "natural" at getting along, such a person is only one in a million. Because it's *not natural* to know how to get along.

And yet very, very few people understand that. They look at someone like Lauri, and they think, "If she can get along like that, there must be something wrong with me because I can't."

And that brings us to a second important fact about Lauri—and the people like her who do get along pretty well. It's this: *There was a time, not very far in the past, when Lauri didn't get along too well, either!*

As a matter of fact, Lauri still has her bad days. No one is perfect. The Monday you just went through with her *is* the rule for Lauri now rather than the exception. But just a week ago last Thursday she had a day like Bert has almost every day.

It only does happen once in a while to Lauri, though. Still, she had to learn it the hard way. She had to make mistakes, admit to herself that she wasn't getting along too well, think things out, try some new ways of acting toward others, and then make a habit out of those that worked. The purpose of telling the stories of Lauri and Bert is so that other young people will have an easier time learning some better ways of getting along with others and with themselves in everyday living.

6 If You Can't Say Something Good...

Bert, unlike Lauri, had his morning start off all right. But then, like a ball bouncing down a flight of stairs, one thing after another had gone wrong until the day seemed like a disaster to him. Yet it really wasn't the day that had gone wrong. It was that Bert had let it go wrong.

How?

The first bad turn Bert had taken was when he talked to Charlie in the hall. Till then, things had gone fine. Bert didn't have to Turn the Boat Around.

But what Bert didn't know was possibly the most important way of getting along with other people: *If you can't say something good, it's almost always better not to say anything at all.*

This guideline can be expressed another way. It's this: *Everyone you meet has something good or attractive about himself or herself. And if you pick out one of those good points and mention it, you'll get along a hundred percent better with him or her.*

Losing the wrestling meet was a bad thing to Charlie. Of course, Bert didn't know the team had lost. If Bert had been really super at getting along, he might not even have asked who won. He might have said something like, "What's new? Anything good happen over the weekend?" Then, if the team had lost and Charlie didn't want to talk about it, he wouldn't have to. He could just answer something like, "No, it wasn't such a great weekend."

But let's say Bert was genuinely interested because he liked Charlie and wanted to form a friendship. So he *did* ask how the wrestling meet came out.

And Charlie would reply that his team had lost. And . . . then came the moment when Bert said the wrong thing to Charlie by answering, "You *lost*? To Overland Park?"

And that was when his day started to go wrong, though he didn't realize it till much later.

Why was it wrong to say that? Because it was negative. Charlie already felt bad about losing, and didn't want to be reminded of it, particularly by an outsider. It would have been different if someone on his own team had said, "We should've beaten those guys."

But why *did* Bert say the wrong thing? It had begun to be a habit with him, and it usually happened for pretty much the same reason. It was this: *Bert wanted to get along so badly that he went overboard in trying to show that he understood the situation.* The situation was that his

[35]

high school wrestling team did seem better than Overland Park. And more than that, in a strange way he was really trying to say to Charlie, "Gee, that's too bad. I think we have a terrific wrestling team, and you're one of the best on it. It just doesn't seem right that we didn't win, does it?"

But Bert didn't say that.

Getting along doesn't always mean revealing your feelings in this fashion. That's hard—you take a risk that the other person won't bare his or hers in the same way, and you'll feel embarrassed. But once in a while it can help.

Yet, with Charlie, all Bert had to do was search for some silver lining in the cloud, look for something positive. He could have said anything from, "Well, you'll get 'em next week," to a simple but sincere, "Gee, that's too bad!"

After that minor but still unsettling conversation with Charlie, Bert's day was balancing delicately between good and bad.

The trouble was, even though he felt this, Bert didn't know quite what to do to swing the balance over to the good. So his day just kept balancing there, threatening to tip over toward being a bad day. And finally it did when he sat with the wrong bunch of guys in Mr. Taylor's class.

After that, everything seemed to turn negative for Bert. He didn't enjoy his other classes much, he didn't much feel like talking to anybody. Still, he wanted to do something to make himself feel better. Unfortunately, when the "scale" of how well you're getting along is tipping the wrong way and you try to correct it all at once by throwing the heavi-est thing possible on the other side, you may hear a crash!

That's what happened to Bert when he went to the pin-ball parlor. He was trying too hard to feel good, wanted the "Boat" of his day to turn in the right direction and make up for lost time all at once! Instead, he ended up being tossed out of the pinball place.

Bert walked around for a while after that. Home was the only place to go, but there his homework would be waiting for him. And he wasn't in any mood to study.

Finally, because he didn't want to have an argument with his parents, he went back to the house. Even then, he was later than he should have been. "You told me you were only going out for half an hour," his mother said to him.

"So it's only nine thirty—what's the big deal?" Bert snapped back.

"The big deal is that when you say something, I expect you to mean it," his mother said. And then she added, more gently, "And I was worried."

"Well, I'm okay," Bert said quickly and hurried to his room, where he shut the door hard. He wanted to say to his mother he was sorry, but he was in too bad a mood.

It took him about half an hour to open his English book. And, after he did, Bert found another fifteen minutes had passed without his really reading a single word. He just sat there, not realizing that he was staring at the page and doing nothing else. He slammed the book shut and started his math homework. That went a little better, but he knew he was multiplying sloppily and might not have all the answers right. About three problems from the end of the assignment, he stopped.

"I just don't feel like doing any more homework," he told himself. "I'll finish these up tomorrow."

It was already near midnight.

Bert got undressed, but didn't hang up his clothes as usual. "What does it matter?" he wondered. "I don't really get along that well in school, and now I don't even have the pinball parlor to go to. Tomorrow things will be worse here because I came home late—and everything just seems like such a hassle."

Bert fell asleep after about twenty minutes, but woke up in the early morning hours. He was having a dream. It wasn't really a nightmare, nothing scary, but enough to wake him. In the dream, he was in the hall again with Charlie, and he knew exactly what he wanted to say, but when he opened his mouth the wrong thing came out again! And then he was in the cafeteria, and he knew exactly what he wanted to say to the girl in line next to him, but he couldn't speak. And then he woke up.

After another half hour of tossing and turning, Bert went back to sleep. But before he did, he thought about the homework he hadn't finished. He knew that he might not get up early enough to complete it.

And he also knew that tomorrow might be another day just like today.

The last thing he thought before he dozed off, though it

was hazy, was . . . "There's nothing so wrong with me . . . a couple of years ago things used to be going pretty well . . . I wonder why everything's such a hassle now most of the time . . . what's the secret of how some kids get along with everybody . . . even their family . . . and I don't?"

7 The Biggest Step

The next morning, when Bert woke up, he didn't feel like going to school. There were too many "Charlies" there. Too many guys in the back of the room in English—and a couple of other classes too—who always seemed to get him into trouble. There were a couple of girls he wanted to know better, but never quite got up the nerve. That was because he'd wondered a couple of times if they were laughing at him, though he knew they could have been laughing at something else.

But he didn't feel like staying home either. It always seemed as though when things weren't going well at school, they didn't go well at home. And they hadn't been going well at school for quite a while. It wasn't the classes themselves, really. Bert was pulling a little less than a B average, though he knew he was capable of better. It was the *people.*

He didn't have a girlfriend. He didn't really have a best friend among the guys. He wasn't a member of an in-group. And he just didn't seem to be the kind of person the other students liked. It wasn't that they disliked him. They just didn't pay much attention. It had been that way for a couple of years, and more and more he just felt like turning over in bed and pretending he had the flu or something.

But he had had the "flu" twice already in the last month and a half. He'd hold the thermometer up to the light when his mother wasn't looking, got it up to 101 or so, and then she'd let him stay home. Beneath it all, Bert felt that his mother knew what was going on, but that she didn't want to push him because she also knew that things weren't the way they should be for him at his school.

His dad seemed too busy to try to do anything about it. They'd had a good talk earlier in the year. Bert felt a lot better afterward, even though his father didn't give advice on any problems. It was just good to know his dad cared for him. It was soon after that, Bert remembered, that he began making a good friend or two in school. But then they seemed to fade away again.

A lot of things he used to enjoy had faded away. Why?

It had happened almost invisibly. "When I was a little kid," Bert thought, "things were easier. Not that I didn't have problems, but lately everything seems to be problems. Why?"

Bert went to school, and nothing much went wrong. Today he did something different—sort of stepped outside of himself and watched himself as if he were another person. It allowed him to relax a little—he didn't feel compelled to go up to Charlie and say something. Instead, he just waved when they passed in the hall. When it came time for the class with that bunch of guys who always pulled him to a back seat and into some trouble, he got there early and sat in the second row. At lunch he waited till the last minute and took his food when there was no one in line and no girl could look longingly at the last piece of pie if he took it.

Bert didn't want any more pain from not being able to get along well with people. "But I can't avoid everybody all the time," he thought. "What'll I do?"

This wasn't the first time Bert had had these feelings. But when he got home from school that day and went off and locked the door to his room and sat at his desk looking out the window, he felt something that was different: "I've just got to do something about it!"

Bert didn't know it, but he'd already taken the biggest step of all. Because, as with just about everyone else who has trouble getting along when growing up, he was at a turning point. Though he hadn't looked at it this way, he had these alternatives:

He could keep on doing the same old thing and hoping it would work, which it wouldn't.

He could decide that there was something wrong with the people around him, which there wasn't, and become hostile toward them, turn into one of the troublemakers at the back of the class and someday perhaps even turn into something worse than that.

He could decide that there was something very wrong with him—which there wasn't. And turn away from people, wait until there was no line at the cafeteria to get his food, and never ask the girl if she'd like the last meat-in-cabbage.

Unfortunately, some people choose one of those false alternatives. They keep having trouble getting along with others because they never stop to think about what they're doing wrong. Or they decide that everyone else is wrong and don't get along because of always criticizing someone or waiting for him or her to make just one mistake so they can say, "Aha! I was right about you!" Or they could simply have as little to do with people as possible. Then of course they won't get along badly with others too often, because they rarely have anyone to get along with!

Bert made the right choice. He pulled away for a day or so to think things out. But he didn't pull away permanently. And he didn't pull away thinking there was something terribly wrong with others—or with him. What he *did* feel was that some of the things he was doing just weren't working out right in his relationships with his friends, parents, and teachers. Yet, because he was doing some things in ways that weren't working out didn't mean he was a bad person, any more than not knowing trigonometry would mean that you were a bad person. It was simply something that had to be learned.

But learning trigonometry was simpler. You took the course, you studied, you asked the teacher if you didn't understand something.

Yet, Bert asked himself, "*How* do I learn to get along better?"

8 A Learning Process

Bert didn't learn how overnight.

But after a few weeks he saw that there were basically just a handful of ways to improve his relations with others, to make people like him better, want to be with him more —as well as to have more fun with them and be more comfortable when he was with them.

The very first way was simply to take a look at what he had been doing and figure out why it hadn't been working. Really, this was pretty much what Lauri did in a situation in which things didn't go right.

Bert noticed, for instance, that it wasn't just Charlie who would suddenly turn off to him in the middle of a conversation. Other people often did. Even his own brother.

Bert went over some of the conversations in his mind— trying to spot that one point at which things started to go wrong. He began to see, more and more, what the trouble was.

And he especially began to see it when he took up a *second* way of learning how to get along better with others.

By observing the people who WERE *successful at all kinds of relationships.*

One of those people was Lauri. It wasn't that he was stuck on her, but he began watching her in the one class they had together, and once in a while in the lunchroom and the halls.

There were others, too. Actually, Charlie turned out to be another. But there weren't many. Bert discovered that not that many people—even older people—had learned how to get along.

And that was the third thing which Bert discovered.

Learning to get along WAS . . . *a learning process.*

Finding that out made Bert feel better. "I'm not that much different from most people," he said to himself. "I just thought I was! Most people are pretty much like me. They don't know how to get along, and they're just pretending to. Or getting in with the wrong cliques so that they belong to something. Or even doing things they don't want, from going out for a sport they really don't like, to going out with someone they don't like, just so they can act like they belong. Or they're pretending to themselves that they give what they want to give, and get what they want to get with other people. *But they don't.*"

Bert learned something else important, too, from that. It was this: If you act as though you know how to get along, but you really don't, you're falling farther behind than if you simply don't get along that well but at least are trying.

Bert tried.

He was far from perfect in the beginning. He was never perfect, in fact, though within just a few weeks he made huge strides, and everyone who had any contact with him noticed the difference.

And liked it.

When Bert began to look into where some of his conversations had gone wrong, and why, exchanges with other people started to go right more often. He discovered several interesting things.

First of all, he realized that people—himself included—talk in code. Or, at least, that's the way he thought of it. It wasn't that they were lying. Rather, they just weren't saying what they meant. They were trying to express one thing by saying another. And it wasn't working.

For instance, he now understood what he'd really wanted to say to Charlie about the wrestling meet—what he *should* have said. Instead, he actually had ended up criticizing Charlie and the team. And that's why so many conversations with Charlie had suddenly broken off abruptly—and perhaps why he and Charlie had never become friends, as Bert had wanted.

But, Bert saw, the code wasn't used only for important questions. It was used, even though people didn't usually know they were using it, in the simplest ways.

Such as saying, "Hello—how are you?"

"I'm not really asking how they are when I say, 'How are you?' " Bert realized. "And they don't think I'm asking how they are. If they did, they'd answer by telling me how they are! But no one ever does."

And yet, Bert thought, the reason that everyone says, "How are you?" is because *they* want to answer the question. That's why it's such a common question and greeting, Bert figured out.

So Bert didn't stop saying, "How are you?" to most people.

But he changed the way that he asked it. Instead of saying the old "How are you?", he *really* asked the question. "How *are* you?" he asked Charlie one day.

Or: "How are *you?*" he answered someone when they asked him, "How are you?"

Or: "How . . . are you?" he asked a girl he would like to get to know better.

On the other hand, if Bert didn't really want to know someone better or spend too much time with him or her, he *didn't* ask how they were. But those to whom he did ask this question started giving him answers. Real answers. When they didn't, he'd repeat the question, say something like, "No—I really mean it. How . . . are . . . you?"

You would hardly believe how much better Bert got along after he learned how to ask "How are you?" and really mean it.

People told him how they were. They told him whether they felt good or bad, of their victories and their defeats.

Soon he was beginning to have almost more people wanting to talk to him than he could handle.

Naturally, it wasn't only from saying, "How . . . are . . . you?" that people began wanting to talk to Bert. He had also discovered the key to some of the codes people used when they talked.

A couple of the most common code messages Bert deciphered were:

"Take it easy" hardly ever meant that. It usually meant something like "I hope you get along all right" or "Stay cool" or "Don't get into any trouble." Or, simply, it meant "Goodbye."

"See you later" didn't mean anything of the sort. Hadn't Charlie said that to him right after he'd told Bert that he *wouldn't* be seeing him later at the pinball parlor? What "See you later" really meant was "Goodbye" or "I'll see you sometime." Bert almost had to laugh after he began to fully realize that. One day his favorite uncle called long distance and signed off with "Well, see you later, my favorite nephew." Bert hadn't seen Uncle Jack in over a year, and he didn't expect to see him for another year! So, actually, "See you later" could also have an affectionate meaning—saying in code that the person *wanted* to see you later.

"I wish I could see you tonight, but I'm fifteen hundred miles away" was really what Uncle Jack meant. But instead of saying that, Bert's uncle had turned a wish into a statement of fact—except that it was a false fact.

Of course, those were things people said every day. Bert

also realized that things people said only now and then—but which were very important—they also didn't mean.

Like, "I love him."

Or, "I wish he were dead!"

A lot of girls, as well as guys, would go out with someone once or twice, or just be in the same class without ever passing ten words and say, "I love him!" or "I love her!" What they really meant was "I've got a crush on her." Or even, "I'm very attracted to that person and wish we had a thing going." Sure, sometimes they did mean love. But was it the kind that was there later in most cases? And they'd use the word love for all kinds of other feelings, such as saying, "I *love* that dress" or "I love anything in leather!"

By the same token, Bert had heard people occasionally say in anger, "I wish you were dead!" They didn't mean it. In fact, they usually felt terribly sorry afterward that they'd said it. What they did mean was something like "I'm as angry at you as I can be!" Or, "One small part of me would like to kill you—or at least hit you as hard as I can!"

Still . . . some people said what they did mean or did mean what they said. Or sometimes they would say part of what they meant or mean part of what they said. And there were times when they would feel exactly what they were saying . . . but wouldn't feel it a minute later! What did it all add up to?

Slowly but surely, Bert began to see that people not only *talked* in code.

Often, even what they felt was in code.

9 People and Cliques

People often aren't sure exactly how they feel about someone or something.

Bert had learned a lot after he saw that the guys and girls around him seldom said what they really wanted to say. He learned that if he *did* say something and *meant* it, people would respond and want to talk to him.

Because of that, Bert learned how to listen better. And people talked to him more and more easily because they started to know that he really was listening—not just letting them take their turn talking so that he could say what he wanted next.

The more someone talked to Bert, the more real feelings began to come out and the code started to vanish.

For instance, there was the time he was walking home from school with Sue. She lived only a block from Bert, but somehow they'd never gotten to know each other because Bert hadn't really gotten to know many people before. Yet now, since he understood how to get along better when talking with and listening to others, he felt secure enough to start a conversation with Sue.

The last couple of days, when he'd sat near her in the lunchroom and a few seats from her in the class they had together, Sue hadn't seemed like her usual self. Usually she was a bubbly person who wore bright colors and seemed to have an optimistic outlook about things. Her nature sort of went with her bright-red hair, Bert thought.

When he noticed Sue walking a few yards ahead of him on the way home from school that day, he caught up and asked how she was.

"I'm okay, how are you?" Sue answered.

"Fine," Bert replied quickly. "But are *you* really a hundred percent okay? I get the feeling you aren't your real self the last couple of days. Maybe I'm way off base, though."

Sue was silent for a moment. "Why do you say that?"

Bert paused. "I can't put my finger right on it," he said as they walked along together now. "It's just something a person gives off—and you always give off a kind of exuberance. Like the color of your hair!"

Sue smiled a little. But then she turned expressionless, which was uncharacteristic of her. "You read me pretty well," she said.

Bert sensed that Sue wasn't saying anything more and it was time for him not to say anything either. That was one of the many things he'd learned about listening. Sometimes people say things through being silent, and Bert had learned to listen to the silences, too.

Yet he also had acquired a good sense of when a silence became awkward. The instant he felt that happening, he said, "Say—the drugstore is just as close as our street. How about a soda?"

Sue agreed, but they took the long way to the drugstore because she found it easier to talk to Bert now. Slowly but surely, she began to tell him what was bothering her. But it *was* slowly—because one of the very first things Sue said was, "You know, something has been bothering me. But I don't know why—it isn't that important to me."

Sue didn't realize it, but her feelings were in code. What she thought was bothering her—that she hadn't gotten the part she wanted in the class play—was only a kind of code for some other feelings she was unknowingly burying. The more she talked to Bert, the more bit by bit she began to tell him and to find out herself what was bothering her.

One thing Bert noticed after he and Sue had talked for about twenty minutes was that she would refer to her mother or father now and then, but really for no reason. When she was talking about why she wanted the other part in the play, for example, she would say, "And I wanted the fiery part of Cathy, because I think I understand that better. My mother's that way." And then Sue wouldn't say anything for a moment. A few minutes later, when talking about a movie she had seen, she would suddenly inject, "I wonder what time my father is coming home tonight. I

wonder if he'll be home for dinner." And then she would go
back to talking about the movie—until she brought one of
her parents into the conversation again out of the blue.

Bert had listened to people enough now to know that no
one said anything by accident. Sue was thinking about her
parents—at least in the back of her mind. Bert didn't push
her, and finally she came out with it herself.

"You know, my mom and dad aren't getting along too
well these days. It really blows me away. It happened once
before a few years ago. They separated for a while, and I
was so happy when they got back together. Gee, I hope
they don't split again. So many of their friends have. I
argue with them a lot—but I'd like them to stay together.
Know what I mean?"

Bert knew, and nodded. It was as if the house you lived
in was your setting and your friends and what went on at
school the main act. But the show didn't seem to go on as
well when the setting was all out of place. Bert had seen a
lot of kids not get along as well at school once something
big had gone wrong at home.

Now that Sue's feelings were no longer in code to *her*,
she talked freely. That *was* what was bothering her! And
she felt better for finding it out, and talking about it to
someone who seemed to care. It was the beginning of a real
friendship between Bert and Sue.

Getting along was not always easy for Bert.

In fact, just when things were really improving—when
he was becoming friendly with Charlie and seeing Sue reg-

ularly—someone really put him down. It was not really just "someone," but an entire group!

Bert had learned very quickly, as most people do once they get the knack of it, how to improve his relationships with individuals. True, once in a while he and someone else didn't hit it off, but then each would steer clear.

But he found that groups were different. First, because there were many different people to deal with at once, it was hard to get a "handle" on any one of them for very long. Someone else would break in with something, and the direction you were going with that one person—whatever you were talking about or doing together—would be interrupted. Yet, second, sometimes the group *wasn't* a number of individuals—or at least it didn't *seem* like it.

Cliques, for instance.

One afternoon, Bert found himself doing a project with a group of fellows and girls who were all on the school newspaper together. The project had nothing to do with the paper, but that was all they talked about most of the time, which made Bert feel left out.

They didn't care. In fact, when he finally tried to ease in by asking one of the girls what something meant, she didn't answer. Instead, she just looked at another girl, who turned and looked at a couple of boys, who turned and looked at the others with a look on all their faces that said, "This guy is really out of it!"

"Well," Bert thought to himself, "you can't get along with everybody, I guess. The main thing is to get the project done."

So Bert ignored their sneers and got down to work. Unfortunately, he couldn't do his part unless the others did theirs. And they were too busy joking and making fun of people. For a while they made fun of someone else who wasn't there—"a real freak" that same girl called the fellow —but soon they found it more fun to pick on someone who *was* there: Bert.

He was the outsider, and they weren't going to let him in. They were using him for their own fun. The more he tried to get along with them, the more cruel they became.

"Hey, how come you never came out for the newspaper?" one of them asked. "Too busy with the circus?"

"Naw," another one said. "Bert's no freak. He's got a head on his shoulders. And it's those little things in life that count!" Everyone broke up.

"Too bad it's on his shoulders instead of his neck," a girl exclaimed. Then everyone broke up again.

The leader of the group held up his hand. "Just a minute, guys and girls," he said. "Enough of this humor at a newcomer's expense. He can't help it if he doesn't understand what we're talking about. And to show I mean that"—the fellow reached into his pocket, took out a quarter, and laid it on the table—"I want to put twenty-five cents toward a brain transplant for Bert."

This time the rest of the group broke up louder than ever, one of them rolling off his chair and onto the floor.

It didn't make Bert feel good. Who *would* feel good with half a dozen other fellows and girls making you the object of their jokes?

But there was another reason that it hurt. It wasn't that long ago—just weeks, really—when this was the kind of thing Bert was always afraid would happen. He hadn't known how to get along with people very well then, and so he'd stayed away from them or said something that would put them off, or talked in meaningless code so that he never actually got very close to anyone or they to him.

Now all that seemed to have changed. Or had it? Wasn't this much worse than having Charlie say "See you later," and not mean it?

Bert wasn't sure what to do for a moment. That part of him which used to be afraid of other people, because he wasn't sure how to get along with them, was scared. Another part of him was angry—wanted to make the same kind of remarks to the six of them that they were making to him!

But now there was a big new part to Bert's personality. And it said to him, "This doesn't make me feel good, but there is nothing I can do about it. And, really, there's nothing wrong with *me* . . . there's something wrong with *them*."

Bert wouldn't have thought that, or at least not thought it strongly enough to have it make the difference, a few weeks ago.

But this wasn't a few weeks ago.

Bert rose from the table and walked toward the door with his part of the project under his arm.

"If a baboon and Bert both jumped off the top of the Empire State Building," one of the girls said with a chortle as Bert opened the door, "which one would hit the ground first?"

"Which? Which? *Which?*" the others all asked.

The girl shrugged. "I don't know—who cares?" she answered.

Bert stood at the door and waited until they stopped laughing. Then, with all the self-control—and some of the new self-confidence—which was in him, he said, "I think I can handle my part of the project without any of you." And he closed the door behind him.

IO Getting Along Means...

An hour later Bert felt good—a kind of peaceful feeling which surprised him.

Sure, a few steps outside the room after shutting the door on those kids he'd felt angry. He'd thought of storming back in and saying what he thought of them! And he'd felt a little insecure again, too. Because one part of Bert still said—and might always say—"What if they're right? Maybe I am a freak. Maybe they're right to make fun of me!"

But that passed, and with it went his anger. Then the peaceful feeling set in.

Part of what helped Bert feel better so soon after a bad scene was that now other people *didn't* act that way toward him. He saw only a few people whom he knew walking through the halls, but each nodded brightly. One of the teachers, in a class in which he hadn't been doing well but was improving, gave him a pat on the back. And when he got home, the whole family seemed especially nice to him. Though, when he stopped to think about it, he realized he'd been getting along better with them too lately. When things went well at school, they seemed to improve at home, too.

But that wasn't the big reason Bert felt peaceful inside. It was something else. It was because he realized that, terribly as everything had gone with that clique from the school newspaper, he *had* gotten along!

How could that be?

The answer was that Bert had begun to see that *getting along* was larger than merely knowing what to say to people and how to say it so that they liked you better. It was more than knowing how to listen to people so that they let you know them better—and perhaps got to know themselves better as a result of you. It was more than doing the right thing at the right time, so that your actions spoke as loudly as your words, and others could depend on you.

Getting along also meant dealing with situations in which there wasn't anything to be gained except to leave the situation as quickly as possible.

In other words, there were some people, sadly, with whom you just *couldn't* get along.

It was much more than the question of whether this was a person with whom you did not *want* to get along.

This led Bert to a whole bigger meaning about getting along.

"Yes," he thought, "there's a much bigger meaning to *getting along*."

Getting along means . . . handling situations . . . coping with crises, not just people.

Getting along means . . . getting along with life.

But what does getting along in life really come down to, if it doesn't mean getting along with people?

For one thing, there was an entirely different group of people from the ones Bert said hello to at school, or the ones he lived with at home, or even those he saw at the pinball parlor or the drugstore. These were the people who made up the "world," if you wanted to call it that. These were the ones with whom you'd probably never have relationships, though perhaps you did business with them once in a while. More likely, you'd see them only once or twice in a whole year or even in your entire life.

But you did have to get along with them, brief as the encounters might be.

Simple politeness was one of the ways Bert learned to get along with the "world."

Bert had never liked phonies, people who went overboard in saying extra things to people they hardly knew or might never see again. On the other hand, he came to see that politeness was like lubricating your car. A thank you in the cafeteria to one of the workers behind the counter, said just a couple of days a week, suddenly made him one of her favorites.

Bert didn't go overboard about it. Actually, he just did

unto others as he would have liked them to do unto him. Take a second and hold a door then, rather than letting it slam when he was coming through next. Little things like that . . . even things with people whom he probably would see only once in his life.

Honesty was as important as politeness, Bert found, in dealing with the world. That didn't always mean being blunt—it simply meant being fair in his dealings with others. One day, for instance, he was given too much change when he bought something in the store. For a minute he was tempted to keep the extra dollar and a half, but as he walked away he started feeling guilty. And he realized that the time he would take thinking about what he'd done, and perhaps suffering from it, was worth a lot more than a dollar and a half. So he went back immediately and corrected the error.

The salesgirl really made him feel good for doing it. "You're one in a million," she said. "This would come out of my check, and my husband's out of work and we've got three kids to support. You're really a doll, honey."

That was worth more than a dollar and a half, too. A lot more. Because moments like these proved to Bert that if he could get along with the whole big world out there . . . he could certainly get along with the kids at school.

11 Health and Time

Most of all, Bert learned to get along in an area of life that had almost nothing to do with people.

Health, for example, was an area of getting along in life that pretty much came down to no one but Bert himself.

He found out it was a good idea politely to stay away from people who came to school coughing and sneezing. And the same went for his own family at home. But in general, staying healthy was more a matter of what he did with his own body. Bert found that if he kept his resistance up, he was less likely to catch anyone else's cold.

And what did he do to keep his resistance up?

Strange as it seemed to him, one by one Bert found he was doing the things that he'd always thought were kid stuff. In fact, he was doing them so automatically—and sometimes enthusiastically—that his parents started to think of him as "our model boy." And gave him extra privileges.

But he wasn't doing it to be a model boy at all. He was cultivating the right health habits because it helped him to get along in the larger picture—not only as a boy, but as someone about to be a man.

Some of the things Bert began doing were:

—Not missing breakfast, and concentrating on a high-protein first meal of the day;
—Brushing his teeth. The mouth and throat harbor more germs than just about any other part of the body, and it's good to clean them every morning (and before you go to bed, too);
—Getting regular exercise outside of school. Bert learned that gym sometimes isn't enough and, even though he was strong from his work in auto shop, his wind wasn't as good as it should have been. So he began trying to work in things like jogging and riding his bike two and three times a week to improve his health "center"—the heart and the lungs. He also sensed that this was a good habit to start early in life, because when he was an adult, there wouldn't be any regular gym class and the outside habits he was forming now would matter even more;
—Making up for lost sleep. Bert realized that sometimes he'd just have to stay up late—or maybe would want to. But he tried to make up for it the next night, even with a catnap after dinner. Work (or play) when you

are refreshed by enough sleep was twice as productive and twice as much fun, he found, than if you tried to plug along when you were tired.

There were more, of course. They ranged from keeping clean (which was part of good grooming) to staying away from junk foods such as too many candy bars, pizzas, soft drinks, and hot dogs.

Most of all, Bert realized that the best *good* health habit of all was not to make *bad* health habits.

Some of Bert's friends smoked, for example, because they thought it meant they were more "grown-up." But Bert had seen the pictures of the "grown-up" black lungs of someone who had smoked for fifteen or twenty years, as compared to the still young-looking lungs of a nonsmoker.

Most of the kids Bert's age also had sampled more than soft drinks, too—and smoked more than cigarettes. But Bert knew there was a difference between simply trying something and making a habit of it.

Bert knew that what seemed cool to many of them today might leave them out in the cold tomorrow.

Time was another area in which Bert learned to get along better.

He'd never really put his finger on it before, but now he saw that he'd often been behind schedule, or hadn't figured out how long something would take to accomplish. Then he'd be disappointed to find out he had no time left to do something else he was anticipating.

He'd often heard people say, "There are only twenty-four hours in a day." Now he began to realize that he'd been acting as if there were twenty-eight hours in a day, or thirty, or sometimes a lot more. That meant he sometimes had to do things at the last minute, and so he didn't do them as well. Or he didn't get them done at all, which would often put him in a bad mood for a while and make getting along with people that much harder.

Then there were the days, particularly on the weekends, when Bert had enough time to get everything done. But there seemed so many tasks (and also so many tempting ways to have fun) that he wasn't sure where to start. Before he'd know it, most of Saturday morning had passed without his beginning a single thing.

Like most students, Bert had an assignment book in which he wrote down homework, appointments, places he had to be at a certain time, and so forth—not counting classes, which he knew by heart.

So what he began to do was not only to put down special appointments, but to make a schedule ahead of time for each day. And for the ordinary things he'd have to do. They turned out to be not so ordinary, and he realized exactly how *not* looking ahead and figuring out his time had been stopping him from getting along better in general.

First, Bert had been allowing from two to three hours for homework each night. But now what he discovered was that on the nights when he had math homework, he needed more time, and the nights when there was no math homework, he needed less. Usually, math assignments were given on Monday and Thursday nights, so he actually could plan ahead not to schedule much else for those evenings, and figure on lighter homework schedules the others.

He also realized that play sometimes took longer than he'd thought, just as work did. The pinball parlor—and the Hamburger Spa—were proof of that. He asked himself, "How many times have I said to myself, 'I'll just jog over and have a quick burger or play a couple of games of pinball'—and before I knew it, a couple of hours had passed?"

One of the big reasons he went to the Hamburger Spa and to the pinball parlor was because there were always some kids hanging around and he knew he'd have somebody to talk to there. Also, who didn't like a hamburger with everything on it? And Bert had become really good at pinball. That was one of his time problems, in fact. On one machine—Planet Wars—he'd become so good that he almost always won free games. He could never forget the time he went to the parlor with just a quarter, and played for over an hour and a half on Planet Wars. The problem was that that was a night he had math homework!

Once Bert started scheduling what he had to do, he began to know better and better how long certain things took. Even when something new came along, he could make a pretty good estimate of how many hours it would require, and fit it in right. This in turn made him more confident about taking on new activities, and he found himself doing more things, meeting more of a variety of people than before. It also led him to drop one or two things which he really hadn't liked that much, discovering they had been taking far more time than they were worth.

Another fringe benefit was that he now found himself having fewer arguments with his parents about what his "rights" were because he had his life more organized and didn't come in conflict with his family as often. For example, if Bert came in too late one night, it was for a good reason compared to a few months ago. He didn't waste weekend mornings as often, either. And when he did sleep late on a Saturday or Sunday morning, he really slept like a log because he appreciated it more now. Everything was pretty much in order, and that's why he felt he could really lie around once in a while and just do nothing.

Scheduling himself and realizing that there were only twenty-four hours in a day hadn't made Bert any different in certain important ways. When he slept until eleven on a Saturday or a Sunday, he was just as lazy as he ever was— and all of us have a lazy streak.

The difference was that laziness didn't get the best of him anymore. It was as though he had almost scheduled *that*, too!

12 What a Clique Is Saying

Once Bert started trying to find ways to get along in all kinds of new situations and with all kinds of new people, he found out something else about groups. Most were what might be called "mixed." In other words, a group—like one individual person with different parts—was made up of people who were relatively easy to get along with, and people with whom it was more difficult to relate. There were those you liked better and those you didn't like as much.

Of course, the reason for this was because groups indeed *were* only this individual and that individual and some other individual temporarily together.

The kids on the newspaper who had given Bert a bad time, for instance, were only a part of the school paper's staff. Bert was a member of the auto club, and one day dropped off an announcement of a contest his group was going to sponsor at the newspaper office. He was a little hesitant about doing it because he thought he'd run into the same six people. Instead, he was happily surprised. Only one of them was there, off in a corner typing; the others, who were higher up on the newspaper, were very polite and warm to him. So you couldn't even judge one group on the newspaper by another group on the same paper!

In fact, the second bunch of kids Bert met on the paper was almost no group at all in the usual sense of the word. They retained their individuality, but were working together for a common purpose. Bert figured that if the same bunch went to a movie together, for the purpose of having fun, they'd keep their identities as individuals in that situation, too. They wouldn't laugh at the same lines, wouldn't all go out to get popcorn at the same time.

The first group of people from the newspaper Bert had encountered might go out to get candy at the same time, and all laugh at the same lines because they had sacrificed much of their individuality in order to be a group. "Maybe that's why they're afraid of outsiders," Bert thought. "They had to try to insult me and make me feel bad." He saw that the reason those six had probably become a group wasn't because they liked working on the newspaper or even because they liked one another. It wasn't a positive reason that had brought them together. It was that each was insecure and negative, and somehow felt more like a complete person when with other incomplete people.

"Not that I'm any complete person," Bert told himself. But the difference was that Bert was trying to build himself up inside rather than tear down other people.

Many groups, though, had *some* weakness. Cliques, especially. That didn't make them bad. It just meant, Bert discovered, that they had to be dealt with or talked to differently.

At the auto club, for instance, you were there because you loved working on cars or tinkering with machines and wanted to learn more about it and try some new things. And you liked to be with people who had the same interest.

Of course there were arguments now and then. But usually someone would argue with another over what was the best way to fit something in or smooth something down. You could pretty much settle such an argument by trying it both ways. Once in a while one of the guys would come to auto club in a bad mood and take it out on the others. But if you pretty much ignored him, did your own thing and didn't get pulled in, it would seldom be a problem. And the fellow in the bad mood might even feel a little better after a while.

What mattered was that—like any individual in any situation—*the group had a reason for being there.* It had a purpose, something to do. If you had the same purpose, knew how to do that something—knew a little bit about how to get along with others—slowly but surely you could become a member of the group in good standing. And sometimes not so slowly.

In a way a clique was saying, "We're all the same kind of people, and we like that kind a little better than other kinds, and that's why we stick together."

Really, Bert had to admit, there was nothing wrong with that. In fact, though some cliques he'd noticed were kind of uncool, there were others made up of some pretty nice fellows and girls. One of those cliques in particular, as a matter of fact, had two or three people in it whom Bert very much wanted to know better. But how would he get in?

The clique Bert liked had about eight or nine people in it.

About was an important word, because this particular group wasn't absolutely tight or closed like some others. Gene and Marty were kind of at the center, along with Audrey and Kim. Often, those four would be together, but sometimes just three of them, if one was busy. When it came to parties or even eating in the lunchroom, though, Joyce, Harriet, and Vic would usually be there. And usually Gary. Sometimes another girl, whose name Bert didn't know, was with the group. The fact that she, and others, were only occasionally with the group was one reason Bert felt he might be able to work his way in.

But the first thing Bert did before doing anything was to think things out—to plan a little. He wanted to be natural once he was with the people in this clique. But right now it wasn't natural for him to be with them at all, so he had to figure out the best way to accomplish that.

The very first thing he asked himself was, "Why do I want to be with them in the first place? Why this group instead of some other?"

Bert didn't have to analyze his choice that much. He liked this group of kids. He was with one or two of them in classes; another didn't live far from him and they'd seen each other around the neighborhood. No doubt whatever they all had in common as people was why Gene, Marty, Audrey, Kim and the others liked one another. Or maybe it was not just things they had in common. Maybe it was differences that, when assembled like the different parts of a car motor, made a complete and functioning unit.

As someone has said, to get to the center of a circle, you have to begin at the outer edge. So Bert began by becoming friendly with Gary and the girl who was only occasionally with the group. Her name turned out to be Sandie. It took a little time, and it took being in the right place at the right time, but soon Bert and Gary were hitting it off pretty well.

Bert didn't push, but he did show an open enthusiasm to talk to Gary and be around him. He acted the same way, though a little bit less because she was a girl, with Sandie. One day during free period, Bert was talking to Gary when Marty and Audrey came along and sat down. That was the beginning.

Bert was a little nervous, but he was pretty much himself. Maybe with another group he would have been hitting his head against a stone wall, but not with this one. For he had learned something important: In order to get along well, you must know with whom you can get along best.

13 Backsliding

One day in May, Lauri and Bert entered the school they attended. They had seen one another casually, and each had a good impression of the other. Bert had always noticed Lauri because she seemed to be one of the more popular girls, nicely self-assured without being pushy. And lately, Lauri had given Bert a little smile when she had passed him because he seemed to be the kind of person she'd like if by any chance they ever got to know each other. "I wonder why I didn't notice that nice guy before?" she asked herself.

That didn't mean Lauri felt she and Bert would become friends or maybe go together.

Lauri knew that was a special kind of relationship, and just because a fellow seemed with it didn't mean she'd be with him. On the other hand, sometimes she might work on a project with him or have a mutual friend, and it would be good to get to know him better then.

Bert didn't feel quite the same, though, when he caught that look in Lauri's eye today. "Say," he thought, "that girl likes me!"

Bert had been getting to know Sue better—so well, in fact, that if she got to the cafeteria first on the three days their lunch periods were the same, the seat next to hers was always empty so he could sit there. And he'd do the same if he got there first.

But the idea occurred to Bert—at least on those days when Sue's lunch period was at a different time—to ask Lauri if she'd like to sit next to him. No, they'd never spoken. "But I think I know how to strike up a conversation with her," Bert thought. "And I'm pretty sure I know how to take it from there now."

Why was Bert so sure that he could be sitting with Lauri a couple of days a week and with Sue the other three?

"Because now I'm someone who knows how to get along with people," Bert figured. "I'm even surprised at how fast I did it."

A couple of other things that happened that day made Bert feel really good.

One was when a fellow from the school newspaper clique, with whom he had tried to do the project, asked if he could talk to Bert for a minute. "Sure," Bert said, but with a bit of hesitation.

"It's been bothering me for weeks," Garth confessed to Bert, "the way we razzed you at the meeting. You know, we kidded about it after you walked out, but after a couple of minutes it wasn't too funny and I think most of us felt like nerds. And I—well, I wanted you to know."

Bert thanked Garth for being honest with him, gave him an affectionate punch on the shoulder, and went on to his next class. "Maybe I'll try out for the newspaper next semester," he thought.

But the nicest thing of all happened after school. A boy a year younger than Bert, someone who had been more than friendly lately, caught up with him on the way home. The boy seemed too timid to speak.

"It seems like you want to say something, but you can't quite get up the nerve," Bert told him. "There's nothing to be afraid of."

"Well," the younger boy said finally, "it's just that I wonder how you do it."

"Do what?" Bert replied, though he felt he knew what the boy was going to ask.

"Oh . . . just know how to make everybody like you and . . . how to get along with them."

What the younger boy didn't realize of course was that just a short time ago Bert too was wondering what the secret of getting along was. But he did tell the guy, whose name was Tommy, some of the things he'd learned. In fact, before he knew it, they were almost to Bert's house, and Bert was still explaining some of the "secrets" of how to get along.

As Bert stood talking to Tommy in front of the house about getting along with people and getting it together in life in general, he began to feel more like a teacher than a student.

And he had another feeling—that Tommy would like to be invited inside. But something stopped Bert from doing that, even though he couldn't put his finger on what it was. Then, when he suddenly saw Sue walking toward them from the other end of the block, he knew what it was: "I didn't want Sue to see me talking to someone a year younger.

"That's why I didn't want to bring him in the house!"

"Gotta go," Bert said hurriedly to Tommy, leaving the younger boy standing alone after he'd spent all that time with him. Instead of going into his house, Bert walked toward Sue.

"Who's your friend?" she inquired.

"Oh, just some kid—I don't even remember his name"— Bert suddenly told this white lie—"from the class under ours. He wanted to ask me something about auto shop." Bert told another white lie.

"Why didn't I tell her the truth?" Bert asked himself. "Should I be ashamed of talking to Tommy?"

And Bert hated to lie. Of course, everyone told lies on the spur of the moment before thinking about it, and he was only human, too. But what he always had tried to do, especially in the last few months, was tell the truth the minute he saw that he'd told one of those impulsive white lies.

This time he didn't. He wasn't ashamed of being with Tommy, but he was a little fearful that Sue might think less of him for talking to a younger boy. So Bert simply changed the subject, and it didn't come up again.

His conversation with Sue didn't last long, because her problems with her parents—and their problems with each other—were really bothering her again. Bert sensed that she wanted to go somewhere and just talk to him about it, like that first day, and so many days since. But today he was on such a high because of everything that had happened, that he simply couldn't get into it.

Later, he felt a little guilty about this, just as he had felt a little guilty about being ashamed to be with someone one year younger. "But I just don't want today spoiled," he thought. "I had my problems and I solved them, and it's not up to me to listen to everyone else's."

But was it really a matter of always having to listen to everyone else's problems, or was Bert being less than honest with himself?

Were his own feelings being expressed in code again?

Whatever Bert's true feelings were about the few moments he had spent with Sue, and about the minute when he'd felt ashamed to be talking to Tommy, they didn't stop him from enjoying the rest of the evening. Too many good things had happened that day. He got his homework done quickly, made himself a sandwich, and settled down to watch his favorite TV program.

"Isn't that something that my favorite TV show should be on tonight, too?" Bert thought happily.

But then he didn't enjoy the show as much as usual. "Maybe it isn't as good tonight as it's been the last few weeks," he thought. "Sure, that's it!"

The next day Bert looked for Sue but didn't see her. He thought about it for a minute, but then his eye caught Lauri walking down the hall and he figured this might be the right day to sit near Lauri in the lunchroom. Even if Sue was in school, their cafeteria times weren't the same, so there wouldn't be a problem, would there?

Lunch hour came, and Bert hurried to the cafeteria. Lauri was popular, and he knew there'd be a bunch of people wanting to sit with her. That's why he didn't have time to stop and talk with Tommy. The youngster passed him in the hall, waved, stopped—waiting to see if Bert would stop and talk—but Bert just waved back and rushed on. Bert didn't feel completely right about it, but put it out of his mind. He was thinking about Lauri. *She* was someone to *get along* with!

Bert was one of the first to enter the lunchroom, but he didn't get into line. Instead, he picked up a tray and went off to the side near the water cooler, waiting.

A couple of minutes later he saw Lauri and a couple of other students walking toward the cafeteria. Bert paused until just the right moment, then stepped into line at the same time they did. Lauri was in front, with one other girl behind her, and then Bert. He made sure he had the exact change ready so that he wouldn't take too long at the checkout counter—and take any chance on Lauri's table filling up—but an opportunity presented itself before that.

Lauri was fishing in her purse for the exact change—maybe she didn't like to carry pennies around, either!—when some coins fell to the floor. Bert was quick to pick them up and hand them to her. She thanked him, and he merely smiled and answered, "No problem." Then he paid his check quickly and caught up with her just as she was picking out a table with her girlfriend, and said, "Say, don't you have one of the leads in the class play?" Sue had told him about that. When Lauri answered that she did, Bert said he'd like to talk to her about something.

"Why don't you sit down?"

He did so and asked if there was a real wind-machine for one of the scenes. He had made it his business to spend a half-hour skimming over the play which would be presented. One big scene, in which Lauri had a lot to say, took place on a windy field.

"No." She felt complimented that he knew she was in the play. "I'm afraid we don't have anything as sophisticated as that. The audience will just have to imagine the wind."

"Maybe they won't," Bert said.

"How's that?" she asked.

Bert told her there was a machine in auto shop which—and he explained it technically—could be made to produce the sound of wind with just a couple of things done to it. He said he'd be glad to fix it to make the desired sound.

"It sounds great!" Lauri exclaimed. "I mean, you'd have to check it out with Miss Faulkner, but it sounds great."

The table had filled up by then, as Lauri's table always

did, and other people began talking to her about other things. Bert fell silent. He'd struck up an acquaintance with Lauri and found a reason to go to the play rehearsal and see her again. When he went to rehearsal he told the drama teacher about his idea, which she liked, then stayed to watch Lauri on stage. Afterward she and he talked some more.

It was natural the next day for Bert to hurry to the lunchroom again and take a place at Lauri's table. There was only one problem. A couple of minutes later, Sue walked in.

14 Give and Take

Bert didn't know what to do. For the first time in a long while he didn't have the faintest idea how to get along in a situation.

What he didn't realize was that he didn't have any idea because he had put himself in this position. He had fallen into the trap of confusing *getting along* with *manipulating*. In other words, instead of reacting honestly and perceptively and assertively toward other people, Bert had begun *using* them. Instead of seeing them as individuals, he was treating them more like one-dimensional beings. And that "dimension" was what *he* wanted from them, not what *they* totally *were* as people.

It was fine for Bert to notice that Lauri seemed to like him. It was all right for him to think of a way to get to know her whereby he could really be helpful at the same time. But was his intention really to get to know Lauri—or was it more to have a popular girl to sit next to in the lunchroom the days when Sue wasn't there?

And what about Sue? There was a time not very long ago when Bert would have been delighted to have someone like Sue to sit with in the cafeteria one or two days a week. Was it fair to her—to his friendship with her—that she should walk in and find him sitting there with Lauri?

Bert had treated Tommy in a one-dimensional way, too. Just as he unthinkingly had put aside his relationship with Sue to sit with Lauri that second day, so he had tossed Tommy aside when he had seen Sue coming down the street. Bert had used the youngster merely as an audience. But again, unthinkingly.

Was it wrong for Bert to feel a bit funny about talking to someone a year younger? Frankly, no. It's a feeling that's only human. On the other hand, Bert didn't like it when he was treated like a kid. And, more importantly, if Bert did feel funny about being seen with Tommy, then he shouldn't have kept talking to the boy until they were standing in front of Bert's own house.

In a way, it was as though he liked Tommy not for what the boy really was, but only because Tommy was an audience. If he had liked Tommy as an individual, or even cared about him simply as a human being enough not to hurt his feelings, Bert wouldn't have snubbed him just because the boy was a year behind him in school.

Perhaps most important of all, Bert had forgotten one of the insights he'd learned about getting along: *The way you think about other people is often the way you actually think about yourself.* And the way you act toward them is either *the way you're afraid they'll act toward you* or the way you *want* them to act toward you. Bert had thought Sue might put him down for talking to Tommy. But would Sue have done that? The truth is that Bert had no reason to think Sue would feel less toward him because he was talking to someone younger, especially when it was in an older-brotherly way. It was really Bert who was putting himself down for talking to Tommy.

Then why did he talk to the boy in the first place?

Because, again without thinking about it, Bert was trying to get something for nothing. He wanted Tommy's admiration, the pleasure of being in the role of someone who knew something and was talking about it. But he really didn't want to be seen doing it.

Getting along almost always involves a give-and-take. Even if it's just getting along in life by brushing your teeth so you don't get cavities, the time has to be given to it in order not to have to go to the dentist.

Relationships especially are made up of give-and-take. That doesn't mean Bert had to compromise what he believed. The hour he spent with the clique on the newspaper proved that. They wanted only to take, and give nothing. So Bert simply got out, sensing that the best way to get along was not to get along with them at all.

But it wasn't the same with Tommy. Bert *had* been given something. Yet the moment he saw Sue, it was as though he stuffed what he'd been given in his pocket and rushed off

[85]

without even saying thank you, let alone giving anything in return. Of course, Bert might have felt that "In return, I gave him advice about getting along." But Bert hadn't gotten along too well with Tommy, so how good an example of his advice was their *own* experience?

And what about Sue?

Bert had dropped Tommy cold to rush over to her. But when Sue started laying a problem on him, Bert just couldn't get into it. Not only did he lie on the spur of the moment about Tommy, but he wasn't willing to really listen to Sue the way he had in the past—the way that had made her a friend. But did Bert always have to feel like listening to someone else? Certainly not.

There are times when you don't feel like giving, when you don't feel like listening. But the point is: *Bert wasn't really straight about it.* He could have said, "Sue—you're a real friend. And I care. But I've got something else right now. Could I call you later and we'll talk?" Or anything like that—anything that was honest, but at the same time showed he cared about the *whole* person, even if he didn't feel like expressing it in a particular way at that particular time.

What it all added up to was that, for some reason, Bert suddenly wasn't getting along too well. That's why he hurt Tommy's feelings when he didn't have to.

That's why his own feelings about not discussing Sue's problem had been expressed in the code of feeling that he shouldn't have to "listen to everybody's problems." What he was really hiding from was the feeling that he was falling into a trap of doing the very thing that had made him unhappy in the first place, yet fooling himself into thinking he was doing the right thing!

Just as getting along better leads to more of the same, fooling yourself leads to more of the same. Beneath it all, Bert felt that. It was why he didn't enjoy his favorite TV program, much as he tried.

And that's why the very next day, instead of giving Sue a call later the night before or trying to find her on the way to school or waiting for her in the lunchroom, he rushed in to sit next to Laurie.

But when Bert saw the look on Sue's face as she entered the cafeteria, he knew that he wasn't getting along that well with her. And, though he didn't know it then, he wasn't getting along that well with Lauri, either.

15 Circles Within Circles

After school Bert had to make a decision.

He'd been working on the wind-machine, and had it almost ready. He could finish it up and bring it to the play's rehearsal before they called it a day, have a chance to show it to everyone and talk to Lauri again—and this time perhaps walk her home.

But he also knew that Sue had wanted to talk to him, and he'd let that go now for more than a day. If he didn't walk her home after school, another day would pass before they'd see each other again. She was obviously going through a tough time again. "I guess I didn't make it any easier by sitting next to Lauri in the lunchroom," Bert thought. It would have been easy enough for Bert to come in later after Lauri's table was crowded as always, give her a big smile, sit someplace else, and save a place for Sue. There were a number of ways of handling it—of getting along with two friends such as Sue and Lauri. But he more or less blinded himself to the situation, hoping it would work out somehow.

He found Sue right after school, and asked her if he could call her that night. She said, "Sure," but there was no doubt her attitude toward him had changed a bit.

"I know there's something bothering you," he said, "but I made the wind-machine for the play and I've got to take it there now—"

"Forget it," she said. "Call me later if you feel like it." There was an edge to her tone that troubled Bert. "I'll make up for it later," he told himself. "I'll try and make up for it when I call her."

"I'll call you!" Bert yelled out to Sue again as she was walking down the hall. She didn't turn around.

When Bert got to the auditorium, there were a number of people backstage. He recognized one as a guy who often sat at Lauri's table, and it made him uneasy.

Still, he demonstrated the wind-machine and everyone, including Lauri, was enthusiastic about it. When the rehearsal was over, though, Lauri seemed to shy away from Bert a little when he joined the group around her. All at once he realized why. She was going to be with one of those guys afterward—probably Dan!

Suddenly Bert began to see a lot of things. Lauri did like him, but that didn't mean he was her boyfriend. Getting along with someone didn't mean that you had a fast friendship. She did have a fast friendship with Dan, however. They had probably known each other a couple of years.

The proof came later when Bert decided to bow out of the scene with good grace. He took the wind-machine, told them he'd be ready with it whenever the play was going into final rehearsals, and said goodbye. Everyone was cheerful to him, and Lauri in particular told him thanks again for going to so much trouble to make the play better.

After Bert had gone, Dan told Lauri, "I think he kind of likes you."

Lauri nodded. "He seems like a nice guy," she replied. And her tone told Dan two things. First, she liked Bert as a person. But, second, she didn't like him in the way she liked Dan—though Bert might have thought she did. "I don't think he likes the real me," she added.

Lauri had done something vital in that moment—and before, too, though Bert hadn't realized it—which is so important in relationships. *She had identified and separated her different feelings toward different people.* And she'd figured out their feelings toward her.

Bert had made the mistake of feeling that because Sue was beginning to feel a certain way toward him, Lauri might also. Again, this was mainly because he had fallen into the trap of thinking of people not really as individuals, but as one-dimensional objects.

Sue smiled at him, so Sue liked him very much. Lauri smiled at him, and therefore did Lauri like him very much? Not necessarily.

Lauri might like him very much in time, though it's hard to have exactly the same kind of relationship—get along in quite the same style, in other words—with all kinds of different people.

Lauri knew that you could indeed have many friends, but each was a different kind of friend.

Audrey, for instance, was someone to whom Lauri could tell just about anything. The two girls had known each other for years and trusted each other completely, though they did have an argument now and then, as almost everyone does.

Then Lauri had another friend whom she actually saw more often than Audrey—Kate. They lived near each other, and Lauri sometimes had a lot of fun with Kate. Yet they weren't as close as Lauri was to Audrey.

And, of course, there was Dan. He was a different kind of friend because he was a *boy* friend.

If Lauri had thought of her relationships as a target with a large circle on the outside, and then a slightly smaller circle within that, and so on until there was one small circle at the center, Audrey and Dan would have been at the center along with Lauri's mother.

In the circle next to the center would have been Kate, Lauri's father, and her little brother. It was not that she loved the people in the inner circle more than the people in the next circle, but at the center was the most intimate circle. Those were the people who knew the most about her, cared to know the most about her, and toward whom she felt the same.

The third circle was made up of most of the other kids she sat with in the cafeteria, her drama teacher, and a few other people. And the circle outside of that included those whom she might call "acquaintances," and some of her relatives. And so on, until there was finally an outer circle of people whose faces she knew and would say hello to, and they'd say hello to her, but they really had never spoken many more words than that and might not even know each other's names.

If one of these people in the very outermost circle smiled at her or said more than hello one day, that might move them in one circle. After all, there was a time when she and Audrey, and Dan too, had only said hello to each other and hadn't even known each other's name.

So, for Lauri, there were all kinds of different relationships and perhaps a dozen different circles of people in her life. And though, by no means did she put her feelings through a computer, it took a lot for someone to even "skip" one circle. Not that Lauri didn't like to make new friends —she did. And she liked people to like her.

But she knew that even when you liked someone automatically, just because the feeling was "there," the relationship had to catch up with whatever feeling you had. And that took time. Or, sometimes it could happen fast, if you went through some kind of an intense experience together.

As a matter of fact, the play was shaping up that way. Lauri had grown very close to her drama teacher now, and to a couple of the other kids in the production. Whether or not those relationships would last after the play was over remained to be seen.

But whatever Lauri felt toward a person seldom changed more than one step at a time, two at most. And her behavior matched her feelings. She sensed that getting along with others wasn't only knowing whom you could get along with, but knowing *in what way* you could get along with each person.

One of the experiences that had taught her this was when her older sister's best friend had run for student council president last year. Betty, her sister's pal, was pretty nice in private, but she lost her cool when it came to trying to get votes. She tried to be on a first-name basis with everyone, and to make a friend of just about everyone she talked to in the three weeks before the election. The boy who ran against her, Tug, hadn't done that. He'd been warm, but if he didn't know people's names, he didn't pretend that he did. And sometimes he didn't ask, but instead talked more about what he thought should be done to make the council and the school better. In other words, Tug hadn't "tugged."

He won by about a 3-to-1 margin.

So one of the things that getting along with others meant was being friendly and even warm . . . but only to the extent to which it was appropriate to be friendly and warm.

When you wanted people to be friendlier and warmer to you, it was so that you could be friendlier and warmer to them. You had to make the relationship firmer so that it could hold that warmth and greater intimacy.

16 When Do Things Start Going Wrong?

For the first time in a long while Bert had the impulse to get lost.

He wanted to leave school as quickly as possible, for it hadn't been good to him today. Then he wondered, "Or is it that I haven't been good to it—which amounts to the people in it?"

He went down the steps, turned in another direction from where a bunch of students stood, and began walking. He found himself headed toward the pinball parlor, sure that Mr. Washburn had forgotten the time he'd kicked Bert out. But as Bert rounded the corner and the pinball place came in sight, he paused.

He still loved to play, and he'd do it again. But was now the time?"

"I'm doing this to escape," he thought. "What am I escaping from? Won't it be there after I play pinball?"

Bert turned around and walked back to the school, hoping he'd find someone from his own group still there. The only one he found was Gary.

"Hey, stranger," Gary greeted him.

Bert was happy to see Gary, realizing that the reason Gary had called him "stranger" was because, though Bert had made a great start in getting in that clique, he'd let it drop during the past few days when he became interested in Lauri. He wanted to make up for lost time now, but he saw that Gary was busy.

"Well," Bert said, "You've got a lot to do, Gary, and I've got to study for that history test. Look for you in the lunchroom tomorrow?"

Gary smiled. "Right," he answered.

Bert felt a little better. He decided it was time to go home and hit the history book. But first he should call Sue. No, he'd go to her house.

When he rang the bell, Sue's little brother answered. "She's on the phone—she's been on a long time and maybe she'll be on a long time more," he said.

For an instant Bert thought of asking Junior to tell Sue he was there, but then he realized he didn't have the right to do that. Not now—not after the last couple of days. "I'll call her later," Bert said.

He went right home and called Sue, but the line was busy. So he did hit the history book hard.

[95]

He felt better when he'd finished it an hour and a half later, but this time he had to wait for the phone because his father was making some business calls.

Bert had gotten into the habit of standing around when someone else was using the phone in the kitchen so they'd know he wanted to use it. This time he didn't. He knew his father was on an important business call, but even if it hadn't been, Bert realized that standing around while someone else was talking so they'd hang up sooner wasn't the best way to handle things.

He was surprised when his dad came to him just a few minutes later and told Bert that the phone was free. "Thanks, Dad," Bert said. "By the way, do you have any time this weekend? I'd just like to chew the fat with you."

Bert's father's eyes brightened. "I'd like that, Bert. Sunday's a good day—maybe we could tinker with the car together—you'll be driving one of these days, you know—and I think you already understand more about cars than I ever will."

Sue's line was finally free.

The conversation was a little strained in the beginning, and Bert knew why. Still, he liked Sue and knew she liked him. If he were up front with her, he felt they could reestablish their old understanding.

"Look—I'm sorry," Bert finally admitted. "I don't even know why I was like that yesterday. I don't know why I've done a bunch of things lately. But I'm sorry I did them. I guess I'm just new to certain things. But I do want to hear what you were going to tell me the other day . . . if you still want to tell me."

Sue was silent for a little while. Then she said, "Yes, I would like to talk to you. But not over the phone. I've really hogged the phone today."

Bert saw an opportunity to tell her he cared enough to come over. "Yeah, I know," he kidded. "I came over before, but your little brother said you had been on the phone for a couple of years and might be on for a couple more!"

Sue laughed. "I was. But do you know the funniest thing —the girl you were sitting with in the lunchroom, who got the part in the play I wanted? Lauri? She's the one who called, and we just talked and talked."

"I didn't know you were friends with her," Bert said.

"I'm not—or I wasn't, anyway," Sue answered. "I think she always felt bad that we both didn't get the part, if you know what I mean. And she was always looking to make it up to me. Strange that she should call today. Because I was really down."

That was a real surprise to Bert—that Lauri would call Sue. Bert learned something from it. But he had an even bigger surprise in store when he met Sue and they walked and talked. The reason she was down and had wanted to talk to him yesterday was because it looked as if her parents were going to split up. "I don't even know if I'll still be living here and going to the same school," Sue said.

It was a pretty heavy scene for her. Bert knew there wasn't much he could do to help—except listen. He wished that he had listened yesterday.

Why had Bert gone wrong for a while?

Sure, he'd figured out where he'd gone wrong in getting along with people and he'd taken some steps to "Turn the Boat Around"—just as Lauri had finally Turned the Boat Around with Sue this afternoon.

But if he didn't know *why* he'd fallen into the trap of letting his attitude toward people change, it might happen again and again. And next time maybe the bridges couldn't be mended.

Bert tried to think back, as he had a couple of months ago when he first attempted to analyze why he wasn't getting along, and pick out precisely where the chain reaction began that made him more a manipulator, or user, of people than a friend or relater to them. He remembered feeling something when Tommy talked to him, but no, it was before that. Was it when Garth came to him and apologized for how the newspaper clique had acted? No. Could it have been when Lauri smiled at him?

It took Bert a long time to begin to see the truth. It wasn't Lauri's smiling at him that had made things go wrong. It was something within himself, and she only set it off.

But what was it?

17 Something You Are

Bert found enough of the answer to help himself and not let it happen again—at least not happen as it had in the past couple of days. But he did not find out completely why, and that in itself was an important answer. He finally realized:

Getting along is not something you learn to do and then know how to do always, like mathematics or fixing an auto engine. Getting along is something you keep learning— something you keep doing.

Bert saw that where he went wrong was when he decided he had learned all about getting along and could take for granted that he always would be right. Getting along, he realized, is something you have to keep working at, every day, again and again.

In that respect, he saw, getting along is like a car motor.

You have to keep putting in oil; make sure that old parts are replaced with new. You can't put the key in the ignition day after day and assume the car is going to start and run perfectly unless you give some time and work to that engine.

What it all added up to in one way was that Bert had made the mistake of living off the results of the "getting along" he had already done. It was as though getting along was money he had put in the bank. Day after day, for a number of weeks and even months, he kept depositing. Then one day he didn't put anything in, but instead made a withdrawal. And another. And then another.

Suddenly he was close to not having any money in the bank.

Yet Bert asked *why* again. He went one step behind the answer he had just figured out, and asked himself: "Why, when I did have so much in the 'bank,' did I start taking it all out and squandering it?"

The answers to that came pretty fast.

First, all of us have the all-too-human impulse not to plan ahead but to enjoy ourselves right now. It's like driving the motor at top speed even if you aren't sure how much oil is in the crankcase. You just hope the motor doesn't give out.

The important thing about getting along, Bert found, was that even if you didn't do it right one day, you could do it right the next. Making mistakes was only human. But if you could make them, you could correct them. There were no final grades when it came to getting along in life or with other people.

Every hour, every day, you were constantly earning a new grade. For a person like Lauri, Bert thought, it would pretty much always be an A or a B-plus. Then it occurred to him that Lauri worked at it harder than he and had been trying longer.

What Bert would soon begin to see is that once you do work long and hard at getting along, you form habits. Thus, working at it becomes such a habit that you couldn't flunk a course in "Getting Along."

Finally, he would discover that getting along isn't something you do. *It's something you ARE.*

Because *getting along* was not just a way of *getting* something. Really, it was more like giving. Only what you gave was your real self. Whether you were holding the door for someone you didn't know, or talking to someone you cared about a lot, it didn't feel right—and it didn't work out right—unless you really meant it.

"It's even true about brushing your teeth," Bert thought. "If you really were into it, you'd get less cavities. And if you only held the door halfway or cared about someone important halfway, your relationship with that person would become muddied. People sense if you're really being yourself, if you actually care about them as human beings. If you do, they give you the same realness in return." Cop. 4

So, Bert figured, "*Getting along* isn't just a way of having

[101]

others care about you. It's a reward you gain when you genuinely care about others."

It was the last week of the semester. Bert was leaving his last class before lunch. He'd just taken a test, and felt he had done well. This was his toughest course—history—and if he could get a B here, his average would be better than last semester.

In the hall he passed a number of people he'd gotten to know. Charlie waved at him and asked what he was doing over the weekend. "I'm not sure yet—a couple of things I *have* to do," Bert answered. "Can I call you tonight?"

"Sure thing," Charlie said.

In the lunchroom Bert sat at the table with "his" group. He'd passed Lauri—she was sitting at another table—and she smiled at him. He smiled back.

Bert enjoyed lunch a lot, and his afternoon classes went smoothly. He felt good, and was thinking of getting a job as a lifeguard that summer. But he had also been offered some apprentice work in a local auto shop, so that was a decision he would have to make.

This weekend he *did* have a couple of things he had to do, though school was over. But he also had a couple of things he wanted very much to do. It would be good to see Charlie, but he wanted to spend as much time as he could with Sue. It looked as if she really would be moving away. It would be hard to lose a friend like her—they'd gotten to know each other really well—but they were going to write. Bert felt they would be friends for life.

As he left the long corridor, opened the big glass doors, and walked out onto the steps of the school's front entrance, he heard someone call his name. It was Tommy.

For some reason, Bert now didn't feel ashamed anymore to talk to someone younger. In fact, once or twice in the past couple of months he'd stopped to say hello to Tommy. But the younger boy seemed shy after the way Bert had snubbed him in front of the house that day.

Now, however, Tommy asked, "Got a minute?"

"Sure," Bert replied. "More than a minute. Why don't we walk on home, and you come inside and we'll have a snack."

Tommy looked at him with surprise. "Gee, that would be great."

When they were on the way to Bert's house, Tommy, after being silent for a while, said, "Remember that talk we had?" Bert nodded. "Well," Tommy went on, "you said a lot of good things, but I just haven't been able to make them work. I was wondering if you could tell me some of them again, weird as that sounds."

"It's kind of weird you should say that," Bert told him. "I don't think I said much of anything that day, except to hear myself talk. And I'm not sure I have that much to say when it comes to what you want to know. It's just a matter of being yourself, and letting other people see it, I guess. And trying to see *them* for what they are. Like—instead of me talking—why don't you tell me what's *really* on your mind? Sometimes things are easier than you think—I'll tell you that. Although if you're like me, you can make 'em pretty

[103]

hard on yourself sometimes!"

Both laughed.

Then Tommy started telling Bert a couple of the things that were bothering him. Bert listened, interested. By the time they got to the house and went inside for the snack, Tommy said, "You know, Bert, maybe you're right. I don't think I have such big problems after all."

"For what it's worth," Bert said offhandedly, so as not to fall into the old trap, "I think you're doing just great—except for one thing."

"What's that?" Tommy asked.

"I'm starving," Bert said. "Let's get that snack!"

"Right on!" Tommy exclaimed.

They were both getting along just fine.

The Authors

Dr. J. H. Schmidt lives in Highland Park, Illinois, and has had a private medical practice for more than twenty-five years. The knowledge he expresses in *Getting Along* comes from his work as a practicing physician and his observations as the father of two children. He has published numerous articles and scientific papers.

Paul G. Neimark is a free-lance writer based in Highland Park. His two previous books published by Putnam's are *Cycle Cop* and *The Jesse Owens Story*, written in collaboration with Jesse Owens. He is also the author of the popular novel *She Lives!*